PIANO | VOCAL | GUITAR ■ CD   VOLUME 86

PIANO PLAY-ALONG
BARRY MANILOW

D0504043

ISBN 978-1-4234-8842-2

HAL•LEONARD®
CORPORATION
7777 W. BLUEMOUND RD. P.O. BOX 13819 MILWAUKEE, WI 53213

Visit Hal Leonard Online at
www.halleonard.com

CAN'T SMILE WITHOUT YOU

Words and Music by CHRIS ARNOLD,
DAVID MARTIN and GEOFF MORROW

COPACABANA
(At the Copa)

Music by BARRY MANILOW
Lyric by BRUCE SUSSMAN and JACK FELDMAN

Moderately, with a Latin feel

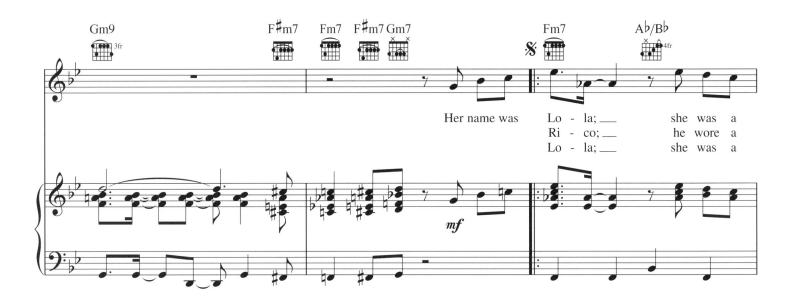

Her name was Lo-la; she was a
Ri-co; he wore a
Lo-la; she was a

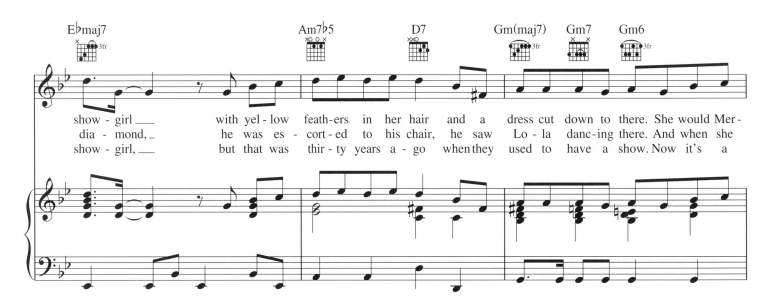

show-girl with yel-low feath-ers in her hair and a dress cut down to there. She would Mer-
dia-mond, he was es-cort-ed to his chair, he saw Lo-la danc-ing there. And when she
show-girl, but that was thir-ty years a-go when they used to have a show. Now it's a

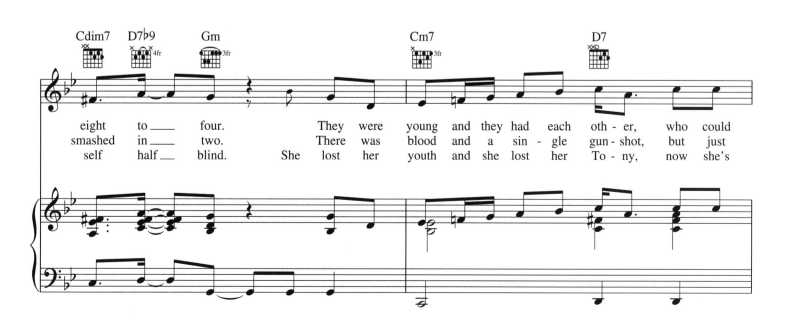

LOOKS LIKE WE MADE IT

Words and Music by RICHARD KERR
and WILL JENNINGS

EVEN NOW

Lyric by MARTY PANZER
Music by BARRY MANILOW

Slowly

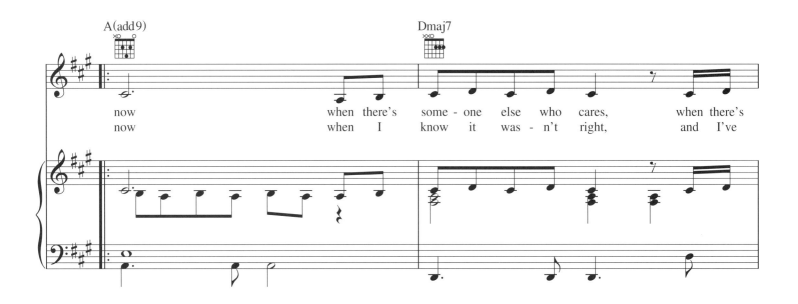

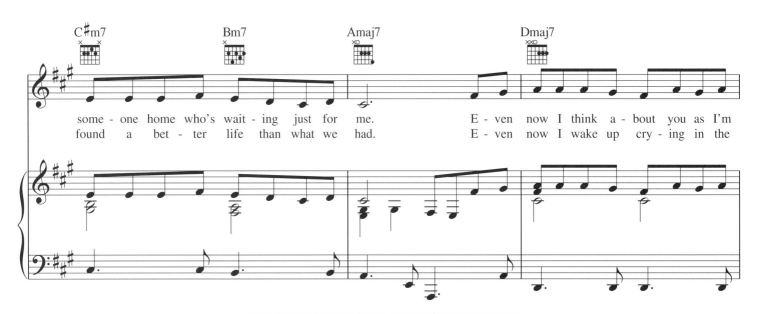

I WRITE THE SONGS

Words and Music by
BRUCE JOHNSTON

MANDY

Words and Music by SCOTT ENGLISH
and RICHARD KERR

READY TO TAKE A CHANCE AGAIN

from the Paramount Picture FOUL PLAY

Words by NORMAN GIMBEL
Music by CHARLES FOX

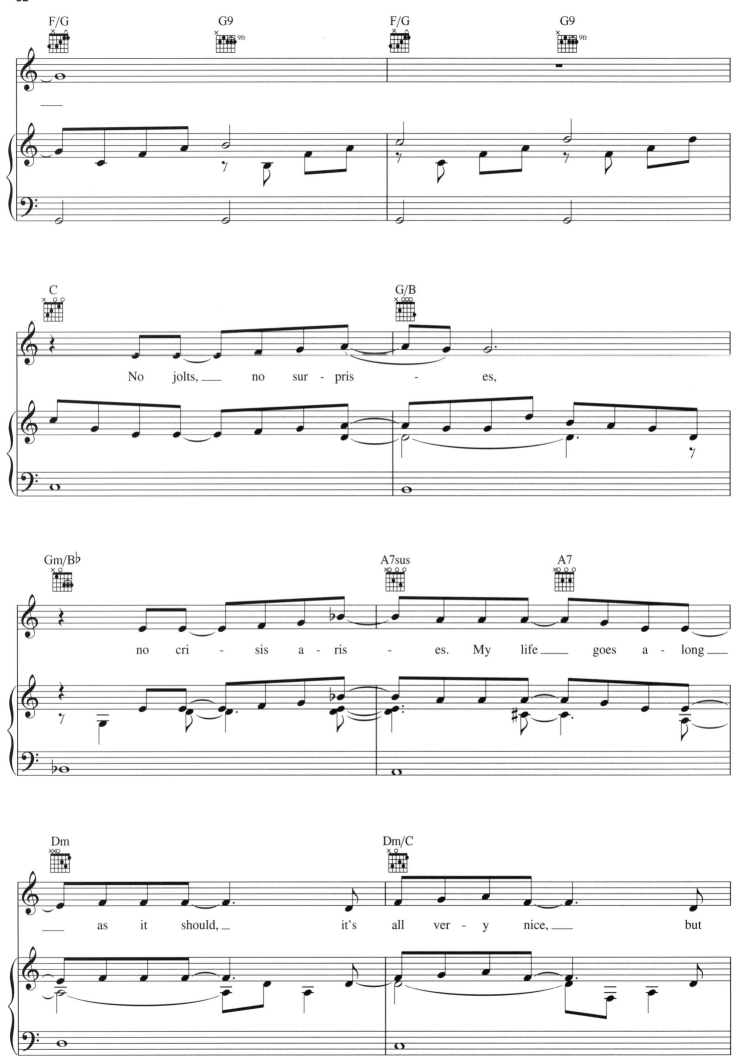

Repeat ad lib. and Fade

THIS ONE'S FOR YOU

Lyric by MARTY PANZER
Music by BARRY MANILOW

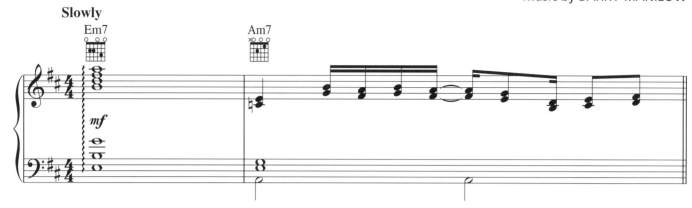

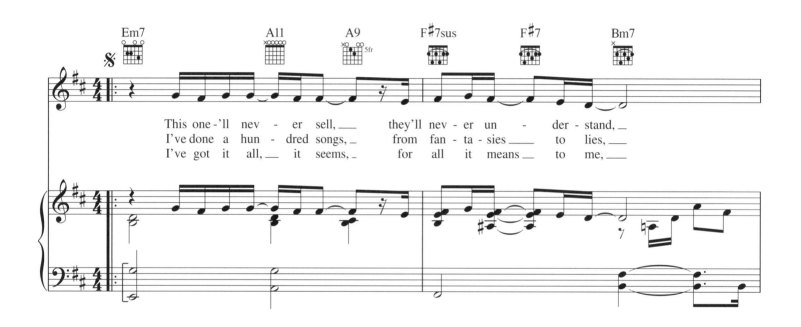

This one-'ll nev-er sell, ___ they'll nev-er un - der-stand, ___
I've done a hun-dred songs, _ from fan-ta-sies ___ to lies, ___
I've got it all, ___ it seems, _ for all it means ___ to me, ___

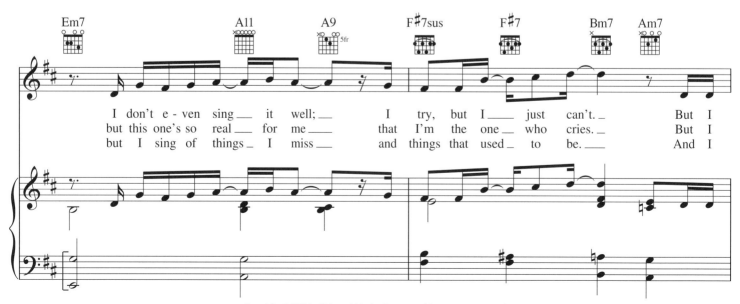

I don't e-ven sing ___ it well; ___ I try, but I ___ just can't. ___ But I
but this one's so real ___ for me ___ that I'm the one ___ who cries. ___ But I
but I sing of things _ I miss ___ and things that used ___ to be. And I

THE ULTIMATE SONGBOOKS

HAL•LEONARD

These great songbook/CD packs come with our standard arrangements for piano and voice with guitar chord frames plus a CD.

The CD includes a full performance of each song, as well as a second track without the piano part so you can play "lead" with the band!

PIANO PLAY-ALONG

1. Movie Music
00311072 P/V/G $14.95

2. Jazz Ballads
00311073 P/V/G $14.95

3. Timeless Pop
00311074 P/V/G $14.95

4. Broadway Classics
00311075 P/V/G $14.95

5. Disney
00311076 P/V/G $14.95

6. Country Standards
00311077 P/V/G $14.99

7. Love Songs
00311078 P/V/G $14.95

8. Classical Themes
00311079 Piano Solo $14.95

9. Children's Songs
0311080 P/V/G $14.95

10. Wedding Classics
00311081 Piano Solo $14.95

11. Wedding Favorites
00311097 P/V/G $14.95

12. Christmas Favorites
00311137 P/V/G $15.95

13. Yuletide Favorites
00311138 P/V/G $14.95

14. Pop Ballads
00311145 P/V/G $14.95

15. Favorite Standards
00311146 P/V/G $14.95

16. TV Classics
00311147 P/V/G $14.95

17. Movie Favorites
00311148 P/V/G $14.95

18. Jazz Standards
00311149 P/V/G $14.95

19. Contemporary Hits
00311162 P/V/G $14.95

20. R&B Ballads
00311163 P/V/G $14.95

21. Big Band
00311164 P/V/G $14.95

22. Rock Classics
00311165 P/V/G $14.95

23. Worship Classics
00311166 P/V/G $14.95

24. Les Misérables
00311169 P/V/G $14.95

25. The Sound of Music
00311175 P/V/G $15.99

26. Andrew Lloyd Webber Favorites
00311178 P/V/G $14.95

27. Andrew Lloyd Webber Greats
00311179 P/V/G $14.95

28. Lennon & McCartney
00311180 P/V/G $14.95

29. The Beach Boys
00311181 P/V/G $14.95

30. Elton John
00311182 P/V/G $14.95

31. Carpenters
00311183 P/V/G $14.95

32. Bacharach & David
00311218 P/V/G $14.95

33. Peanuts™
00311227 P/V/G $14.95

34. Charlie Brown Christmas
00311228 P/V/G $15.95

35. Elvis Presley Hits
00311230 P/V/G $14.95

36. Elvis Presley Greats
00311231 P/V/G $14.95

37. Contemporary Christian
00311232 P/V/G $14.95

38. Duke Ellington – Standards
00311233 P/V/G $14.95

39. Duke Ellington – Classics
00311234 P/V/G $14.95

40. Showtunes
00311237 P/V/G $14.95

41. Rodgers & Hammerstein
00311238 P/V/G $14.95

42. Irving Berlin
00311239 P/V/G $14.95

43. Jerome Kern
00311240 P/V/G $14.95

44. Frank Sinatra – Popular Hits
00311277 P/V/G $14.95

45. Frank Sinatra – Most Requested Songs
00311278 P/V/G $14.95

46. Wicked
00311317 P/V/G $15.99

47. Rent
00311319 P/V/G $14.95

48. Christmas Carols
00311332 P/V/G $14.95

49. Holiday Hits
00311333 P/V/G $14.95

50. Disney Classics
00311417 P/V/G $14.95

51. High School Musical
00311421 P/V/G $19.95

52. Andrew Lloyd Webber Classics
00311422 P/V/G $14.95

53. Grease
00311450 P/V/G $14.95

54. Broadway Favorites
00311451 P/V/G $14.95

55. The 1940s
00311453 P/V/G $14.95

56. The 1950s
00311459 P/V/G $14.95

57. The 1960s
00311460 P/V/G $14.99

58. The 1970s
00311461 P/V/G $14.99

59. The 1980s
00311462 P/V/G $14.99

60. The 1990s
00311463 P/V/G $14.99

61. Billy Joel Favorites
00311464 P/V/G $14.95

62. Billy Joel Hits
00311465 P/V/G $14.95

63. High School Musical 2
00311470 P/V/G $19.95

64. God Bless America
00311489 P/V/G $14.95

65. Casting Crowns
00311494 P/V/G $14.95

66. Hannah Montana
00311772 P/V/G $19.95

67. Broadway Gems
00311803 P/V/G $14.99

68. Lennon & McCartney Favorites
00311804 P/V/G $14.99

69. Pirates of the Caribbean
00311807 P/V/G $14.95

70. "Tomorrow," "Put on a Happy Face," And Other Charles Strouse Hits
00311821 P/V/G $14.99

71. Rock Band
00311822 P/V/G $14.99

72. High School Musical 3
00311826 P/V/G $19.99

73. Mamma Mia! – The Movie
00311831 P/V/G $14.99

74. Cole Porter
00311844 P/V/G $14.99

75. Twilight
00311860 P/V/G $16.99

76. Pride & Prejudice
00311862 P/V/G $14.99

77. Elton John Favorites
00311884 P/V/G $14.99

78. Eric Clapton
00311885 P/V/G $14.99

79. Tangos
00311886 P/V/G $14.99

80. Fiddler on the Roof
00311887 P/V/G $14.99

81. Josh Groban
00311901 P/V/G $14.99

82. Lionel Richie
00311902 P/V/G $14.99

83. Phantom of the Opera
00311903 P/V/G $14.99

84. Antonio Carlos Jobim Favorites
00311919 P/V/G $14.99

85. Latin Favorites
00311920 P/V/G $14.99

89. Favorite Hymns
00311940 P/V/G $14.99

90. Irish Favorites
00311969 P/V/G $14.99